Shake 'Em Up

Introduction

BY AMY STEWART

For two months I occupied an apartment next door to the offices of Tin House, the publisher of this book. I promised to pour the editors a drink if they ever came by after work, and sometimes they did. Because I was living there temporarily, I didn't have a well-stocked bar, so I gave them their choice of an old-fashioned or a glass of straight whiskey. I think

I served them pretzels once, and another time they got almonds. I never had enough chairs. You might think I wasn't much of a hostess, but Virginia Elliott and Phil Stong would have approved.

Let's imagine Virginia and Phil as That Couple Upstairs. You know the type. They never issue party invitations, but most nights people seem to turn up anyway. From their fire escape comes laughter and cigarette smoke and the faint clatter of ice cubes against glass. Sometimes one of them calls down to the delicatessen for a carton of orange juice or a can of sardines, but otherwise they seem to make no actual preparations for their parties. They know that people will drink whatever's on hand and eat any food set before them, even saltines spread with butter and toasted in the oven (see p. 46).

Why are Virginia and Phil so unconcerned about the state of their liquor cabinet or the quality of their canapés? Because they are Prohibition-era hosts, and as such they have far more practical

2

WPK

Published by Tin House Books, Portland, Oregon, and
New York, New York

Distributed to the trade by Publishers Group West,
1700 Fourth St., Berkeley, CA 94710, www.pgw.com

Interior design by Diane Chonette
Printed in the USA
www.tinhouse.com

Shake 'Em Up

A PRACTICAL HANDBOOK
OF POLITE DRINKING

by Virginia Elliot & Phil D. Stong

ILLUSTRATIONS BY HERB ROTH

Tin House Books

Portland, Oregon & New York, New York

recipe for homemade "non-alcoholic gin" has been restored to its rightful location at the beginning of a section called "Household Hints."

Now, about the drinks. You'll notice that these are not complex recipes burdened with exotic or handcrafted ingredients. If you're in the habit of frequenting bars that claim to serve Prohibition-era cocktails, you might be surprised to learn that Virginia and Phil got by with little more than canned grapefruit juice and ginger ale to enliven their "non-alcoholic" alcohol. The recipes are simple, familiar, and unpretentious. The ingredients can be had at any corner liquor store on a modest budget. The measurements are imprecise, and no technique is required beyond a good stir. You will find no dandelion-burdock bitters, flaming orange peels, or Olympic-style shaking here.

The food, as I've mentioned, is so simple that you might call it artless: Virginia and Phil's guests were satisfied with Velveeta sandwiches seasoned with catsup, toasted potato chips with chutney, and cream cheese spread on white bread and topped with chopped peanuts and pickles. Most ingredients could be stored indefinitely in the pantry and simply tossed at the guests when they started to grumble.

In fact, *Shake 'Em Up* is less a recipe collection and more a survival guide for hosts. Our authors assume that you don't just open your doors once a year for an extravagant party; rather that, like them, you suffer an endless parade of thirsty and ill-behaved guests without whom life would be unbearably dull. The primary aim of this book is to teach you how to handle those people. They'll advise you on the care of "tender young things, who have just been taken off stick candy" and don't know how to enjoy a proper adult drink: just gather up crème de menthe or crème de cocoa, "make them up some kind of a mess of it and push them under the piano to suck on it." For the guest who "wants to drink all the liquor he can hold and then pour any possible surplus in his hair," they suggest a cheap mixture of "non-alcoholic" alcohol, water, gin flavoring, and tabasco.

Phil and Virginia know how to shore up intoxicated guests who are called suddenly away to preach a sermon or deliver a speech. For guests who show up late and realize they are two or three cocktails behind the rest of the party, they prescribe hot drinks. "Heat acts on the villi and such things like an air-mail stamp," they pronounce with scientific authority. Hangover cures run the gamut from a cup of milk to Blowing the Brains Out. And they wisely furnish blank pages at the end for recipes and "Idiosyncrasies of Your Friends." (The real reason for the blank pages is that books are most economically printed in signatures of sixteen pages each, and they needed to fill eighty pages to round out five full signatures, but never mind.)

So who are these geniuses, these Nick and Nora types who speak to us from a bygone age in which guests were content with a glass of gin and orange juice and a jar of olives? Here's what we know: Virginia Elliott, born Helen Virginia Fulton in Ohio in 1896, married architect Lawrence Elliott in 1921. They were living in Manhattan when her first book, *Shake 'Em Up*, was published in 1930, but by 1932 they had divorced. Her next book, published in 1933, was *Quiet Drinking; A Book of Beer, Wines & Cocktails and What to Serve with Them*. In 1934 she and Robert Howard Jones, an architect she would marry in 1936, coauthored a book called *Soups and Sauces*. Jones died sometime before 1962, and Elliott lived on New York's Upper East Side until her death in 1977.

It's not clear how she met her coauthor Philip Duffield Stong, but we do know that they were both living in Manhattan and working as free-lance writers at the time. Stong, born in Iowa in 1899, trained as a journalist and worked for the Associated Press as well as other newspapers and

8

magazines. He interviewed anarchists Sacco and Vanzetti just before their execution in 1927, recording what would become a controversial quote about their death sentence: "Our words—our lives—our pains—nothing! The taking of our lives—the lives of a good shoemaker and a poor fish peddler—all! The last moment belongs to us—that agony is our triumph."

Shake 'Em Up was Stong's first book, but shortly after its publication he was at work on the novel that would make him famous: *State Fair*. The book was adapted into a movie starring Will Rogers and another starring Pat Boone and Bobby Darin, as well as a 1945 musical with a Rodgers and Hammerstein score. He went on to write a few dozen novels for adults and children, but none were as popular as *State Fair*. He and his wife, novelist Virginia Swain Stong, lived comfortably in Manhattan and later in Connecticut, boarding a cruise ship for the tropics every few years until his death in 1957 at the age of fifty-eight.

I'm delighted that we've been able to resurrect *Shake 'Em Up* some eighty-three years after its original publication for a new generation of cocktail aficionados. If you've never served gin and hot water to a guest, or smeared equal parts Brie and butter on a saltine and called that an appetizer, or taken a glass of rye and grapefruit juice before breakfast, you haven't *truly* experienced Prohibition-era living. Let Virginia and Phil show you the way.

Shake 'Em Up

THIS BOOK IS ALL WET.

It is made for People Who Fling Parties, People Who Go to Parties, People Who Just Have a Table of Bridge, People Who Don't Really Drink but Feel That a Cocktail or Two Enlivens Conversation—in short, for American People in the twelfth year of Volstead, 1930.

It has taken the authors twelve years to write this book—twelve years of bathtub gin, synthetic Scotch, home-made wine and needled beer. Twelve years is not too long to spend wearing the weeds for the Good Old Days.

13

Till now, their copies of the Bartender's Guide—with tear-stained pages, it is true—have stood dusted and honored on the library table, beside the telephone pad with the name of the Man Who Can Get It Right Off the Boat—and never does.

But now they realize that One Must Go On Living. They have taken down the yellowed tome and wrapped it, with its fragrant freight of Sherry 1820, its Green Chartreuse, its Napoleon Brandy, its Chateau Yquiem, and laid it away with Grandma's Bridal Corset and the Little Shoes of Uncle Ichabod.

In memory of the Bartender's Guide and Many Memorable Parties, they have made a book for the 1930 American, and they offer it to him with a Brave Little Smile.

For him, it has four specific virtues.

1. It is a tactful book. If it recognizes that he is a cripple in the vineyards of his ancestors, it will not

point its finger at his crutches. It will not face him with demands for dashes of nectar and quantums of hydromel. Its formulae are based upon the ingredients now available: non-alcoholic (ignore the prefix at your own peril) Gin, Scotch, Rye, Corn and Applejack. (In case the latter in non-alcoholic form is hard to get, the authors suggest that you obtain some alcoholic applejack, distil it at 78 degrees centigrade, and allow the noxious fumes of the alcohol to escape. Then you throw away the residue and eat the still.)

2. It is an artistic book. Starting on the assumption that Total Unconsciousness is not the goal of Perfect Drinking, it will show him not only what to drink and how, but what to eat while drinking. It will supply him—and the Lady Who Is So Sick of Thinking Up Menus She Could Scream—with scores of recipes for simple but imaginative canapés and other leitmotifs upon which the perfect opus of a Light-Jag can be leisurely elaborated. The cheese daffy-dillys, the olive thingumbobs, the caviar and chutney willy-wallys are apportioned with loving care to just those drinks which Heaven Intended Them For.

3. It is a polite book. The complicated problems of etiquette raised by the passage of the Eighteenth Amendment are solved here. There is a formula for disposition of the guest who arrives cold sober after the party is well on its way. The Bottle for a Certain Purpose is described for the benefit of Him Who Is His Own Worst Enemy.

4. It is a humane book. It suggests preventive and remedial treatment for those unfortunates who re-fuse to profit by its urbanities. It tells what to do for the guest who Knew He Shouldn't Have Mixed His Drinks, for the one who has a Bad Fall while tap-dancing on the piano, for the Clumsy Fool who couldn't broil the goldfish without burning his thumb. If these can be saved, it tells how to save them; if they are sodden in their ways, it tells how to render them innocuous without resorting to the ungentle expedient of the Left Hook.

———◦◦◦———

Commissary

The following list represents an Ideal and should be treated, accordingly, with respectful insouciance. However, admonitions to husbands to "just run down to the grocery, dear, and get this little list of things—it's right in the same block," have often resulted in Broken Necks and the inevitable pause in the party while the body is pushed in the incinerator.

Real Hostesses will feel too strongly the duties of hospitality to wish to miss parties on this account, particularly if Pater Familias finds it necessary to give most of his attention to The Blonde, and neglects the glasses.

Even should Pater Familias not resort to this justifiable violence, adequate supplies in the kitchen will simplify the Hostess's labors and enable her to catch an occasional glimpse of the guests, and sometimes even to take a drink. Let each Reader, therefore, edit this Commissary List temperately, according to her necessities.

Commissary List

6 cans of grapefruit juice

1 case ginger ale

1 case White Rock
*It's cheaper by the case and can be pushed under the
davenport or bed if you have little storage space.*

1 bottle Angostura Bitters
*It last for years if kept in a hair-tonic bottle, and your
drinks will be better. A dash means a dash.*

1 bottle Maraschino
Keep the liquor from the cherry bottle.

1 bottle Grenadine
Domestic has a decent flavor and can be had at any grocery store.

6 bottles of stuffed olives

6 cans of boned and skinned sardines

6 jars pâté de foie gras
Keep this for elegant guests.

1 jar Cross and Blackwell anchovy paste
It is very potent and keeps forever.

1 bottle Major Grey's Chutney

6 small jars peanut butter

6 cans of dry shrimp

1 pint jar of mayonnaise

*This should be home-made, unless you can eat the
store stuff.*

6 bottles of pearl onions

6 jars of black caviar

6 jars of pink caviar

2 jars of prepared horseradish

2 air-tight cans of salted almonds

*If you have them around people will eat them unconsciously
and they* do *oil the stomach, thus retarding immobility.*

2 large tin boxes of ordinary saltines

6 boxes of Cheese Snaks

These are delicious with stirred cocktails or highballs.

3 tins of Touraines

3 boxes of Caviarettes

They have a nice little rim which prevents the eggs from rolling off and staining clothes. Never serve caviar on plain wafers, they crumble too easily.

3 tins of Peak Frean whole wheat biscuits

3 tins of Peak Frean Cheese biscuits

3 tins of Peak Frean assorted biscuits

Cream cheese must be kept in the ice box, and never bought more than one day before using.

All other cheese will keep indefinitely if carefully covered and kept in the ice box.

An Ounce of Prevention

For the Party Which You Know Will Be Too Much For You, certain preparatory measures, less pessimistic than the Making of a Will, may be taken:

A Great Actress eats a can of cold tomatoes.

A quart of milk is a conservative preparation.

A physician recommends a large plate of green pea soup.

A Can of Tomato Juice, highly seasoned with cayenne and black pepper, warns the proper authorities to be on their guard.

A Pony of Olive Oil is reputed to coat the stomach lining and ameliorate the wear and tear of subsequent beverages. (In one case this is known to have failed miserably; the question brought up was, Would anything have done any good?)

A quantity of Moderately Broiled Bacon achieves the same effect.

These should be taken, of course, as immediately before drinking as is practicable. Stomachs are as eccentric as their owners, naturally, and if they don't respond to on of these precautions, they may to another.

—◦◦◦—

Take Four before Meals

If you happen to like your guests and wish to talk to them it is an excellent idea to have the liquid elements of the first cocktail mixed and cooling in the refrigerator before they arrive. Ice cubes or finely cracked ice will be placed in the service bucket and left on the *bottom* shelf of the refrigerator at the last possible moment, since in order to chill drinks quickly, the ice should be reduced to such small fragments that it will melt with rather disconcerting speed if allowed to stand long. The bottom shelf of the refrigerator is always coldest, of course.

There is more than convenience as an advantage in pre-mixing. It gives the non-alcoholic gin, rye or what-not time to get acquainted with the rest of the cocktail. For the same reason, a cocktail should be shaken beyond the time required for mere chilling. Gentlemen who have been disappointed in their youthful aspirations to become orchestra conductors or Indian Club swingers on the vaudeville stage will oblige, without admonition, particularly if you have taken the simple precaution to invite The Blonde.

If Father's Frustration happens to be present, hand the shaker to him, drop a cloth on a tray, spread your canapé mixture on toast rings or wafers, chill the glasses by whirling a piece of ice in each of them, place them in a circle on the tray, take the cocktail napkins from the drawer, slide the canapé platter on one side of the tray and march into the living-room to the mental strains of "Après Midi d'un Faun."

Never ask the Artist of the Shaker to come to the kitchen for his implement, as the rest of the guests are likely to follow him and spoil the triumphal entry. They are also likely to be in your way.

The amount of bread used in a canapé should be measured according to the capacities and tendencies of your guests. If they are the kind who will sit looking poignantly at the empty shaker until you are compelled to make the fifth round, and subsequently to watch the destruction of your dinner service, use plenty of bread. It's good blotting paper.

Coasters are a snare and a delusion. Besides annoying your guests, they are seldom needed and they complicate life unreasonably. Instead of using them, give all furniture in the line of fire a polish of liquid wax before the battle. Then you can say with impunity of your choicest antique, "Oh, put your glass down right on the table. It's an old thing we don't care anything about and it can't hurt it."

If your dinner is going to be pretty good, all in all, serve only two rounds of cocktails and light canapés.

"Adequate supplies in the kitchen will simplify the Hostess's labors and enable her to catch an occasional glimpse of the guests, and sometimes even to take a drink."

—◦◦◦—

Exquisites

For guests who Drink for Flavor, and that infinites-
imal glow which only accentuates slightly the vivid
spirits of good companions, the following cocktails
and their accompanying canapés are recommended. The physiological effects are almost negligible.

....

BRONX COCKTAIL

One part gin

One part Italian Vermouth

and the juice of ¼ orange

Shake with plenty of crushed ice until very cold.
With this serve:

....

PEANUT BUTTER CANAPÉS

Spread round of toast (graham or white bread) with
peanut butter. On top place a small piece of very
crisp bacon.

ANCHOVY CANAPÉS

Spread rounds of graham toast with anchovy butter. Garnish with one slice of stuffed olive.

ROLLED VELVEETA CHEESE SANDWICHES

Cut the crusts from one large loaf of white bread. Slice very thin, the long way of the loaf. Mash one Velveeta cheese with a silver fork, add one teaspoon of Worcestershire Sauce, one teaspoon of catsup, salt and pepper. Spread on the long slice of bread. Cut the bread into three even parts. Roll each one, tie with a string, and toast them in the oven until golden brown.

....

BIJOU COCKTAIL

Two parts gin

One part Italian Vermouth

and one part Chartreuse

Shake with plenty of ice until the ice is completely melted. *With this serve:*

....

CAVIAR AND ONION CANAPÉS
Mix one part pearl onions with two parts pink caviar, add a dash of lemon juice and serve on rounds or diamonds of white toast.

POTATO CHIPS FILLED WITH CHUTNEY
Crisp a box of potato chips in the oven for a few minutes. Fill each one with chutney and serve at once. The chips go limp if allowed to stand.

34

MILWAUKEE SANDWICHES

Trim the crusts from a loaf of white bread. Slice very thin and spread each slice with creamed butter. Put a thin slice of chicken on a piece of bread, sprinkle with grated Parmesan cheese, cover with another buttered slice of bread. Toast on both sides, cut in triangles and serve hot.

....

BOSTON CLUB COCKTAIL

Two parts gin

One part Italian Vermouth

and the juice of one-half lime

Shake with ice and pour into very cold glasses, over a few pearl onions. *With this serve:*

....

CAVIAR CANAPÉS

Spread rounds of thin toast with sweet butter. Over this spread a layer of black caviar. Squeeze over it a little lemon juice and serve.

PIMIENTO CHEESE CANAPÉS

Spread whole wheat wafers with pimiento cheese that has been mixed with a little sweet cream. Garnish with cucumber rings and serve.

WATERCRESS AND BACON SANDWICHES

Spread thin slices of white bread with butter. Press onto one slice a few sprigs of very crisp watercress, add two slices of crisp bacon, cover with another buttered slice, cut in quarters and serve.

ORANGE BLOSSOM COCKTAIL

One part gin

One part orange juice

and a dash of Grenadine

Fill the shaker half full of very fine ice, add the liquid and shake until very cold. *With this serve:*

RIPE OLIVES

The olives must be prepared a day before using. Place large ripe olives in a bowl, cover with olive or vegetable oil, add four cloves of garlic, cover tightly and let stand over night in the ice box. Drain thoroughly, dump onto a towel, dry well, and serve in a bowl lined with crisp lettuce leaves.

PÂTÉ DE FOIE GRAS CANAPÉS

Spread rounds or triangles of toast with pâté, garnish with a curled anchovy and serve.

TOASTED CHEESE SANDWICHES

Melt American cheese in a double boiler. Add Worcestershire Sauce, salt, cayenne, and finely chopped broiled bacon. Toast triangles of white bread on one side, spread the fresh side with the cheese, and toast until the cheese is a light brown. Serve hot.

—◦◦◦—

Shot in the Arm

If you have invited strangers who, you just know, will like each other—and of course, they don't—or if conversation languishes like a Dickens heroine, or if you don't like the party yourself, try these combinations. Repeat doses until cured.

....

BING COCKTAIL

Two parts gin

One part Italian Vermouth

Six white grapes

One part fresh orange juice

and the juice of a lime

Crush six grapes in the bottom of a pitcher. To this add two parts of gin, one part Italian vermouth and one part fresh orange juice and the juice of a lime. Stir well and pour into a shaker half filled with ice. Shake until very cold. *With this serve:*

....

SAVORY CAVIAR

Spread rounds of toast with black caviar. Place in a very hot oven for one and one-half minutes. Serve at once.

CELERY STUFFED WITH ROQUEFORT

Cream one-eighth of a pound of Gorgonzola or Roquefort cheese with as much cream cheese or butter as is necessary to make a thick paste, add one teaspoon of Worcestershire Sauce and a dash of white pepper. Fill tender pieces of celery with the mixture and serve very cold. The mixture also makes a good cracker spread.

SARDINE SANDWICHES

Mash boned and skinned sardines to a paste. Add an equal amount of hard-boiled egg yolks, which have been put through a sieve. Season with salt, cayenne and a few drops of lemon juice. Make moist with melted butter. Spread between slices of thin buttered bread. Cut in thin strips and serve.

....

GRAPEFRUIT JUICE COCKTAIL

One part gin

One part grapefruit juice (a fifteen-cent can is as
good for this purpose as fresh fruit and makes eight
cocktails)

and two teaspoons of Grenadine

Shake until very cold and pour. This is probably
the easiest of all cocktails to make, is very pleasant
to take and is exceedingly potent. *With this serve:*

....

CHICKEN LIVER CANAPÉS

Cook one-half pound of chicken livers (fresh or
tinned) very gently, in butter, for five minutes. Saute
six fresh mushrooms in butter, then chop very fine.
Mix with the livers, which have been mashed up,
add a teaspoon of lemon juice, one of onion juice,

salt and pepper. Spread on salted wafers and serve at once. If allowed to stand they will soak.

PIGS IN BLANKETS

Wrap stuffed olives each in half a slice of bacon. Spear with a toothpick (this serves to hold the bacon on and also as a handle), place on a grill and broil, being careful to pour off the fat as it is rendered and to turn the pigs so that they will be crisp on all sides. Serve hot.

Never serve these to male guests unless you are willing to make dozens.

CREAM CHEESE AND CHIVE SANDWICHES

Mix one cream cheese, one-quarter of a cup of finely chopped chives, half a teaspoon of salt, and one tablespoon of heavy cream. Spread between very thin slices of white bread. Cut in fancy shapes and serve.

....

HAWAIIAN COCKTAIL

Two parts of Applejack (apple brandy, if you can get it)

One part pineapple juice

and the juice of one lemon

Pour into a shaker half-filled with very fine ice, shake well and serve. *With this serve:*

....

SALTINES
Spread with butter and toasted lightly.

DUTCH CHEESE ROLLS
These can be bought at any good grocery or delicatessen.

CAVIAR SANDWICHES

Spread thin slices of buttered bread with a mixture made of half black caviar and half pearl onion. Cover with another slice of bread, cut into triangles and serve.

DRY MARTINI COCKTAIL

Two parts gin

One part French Vermouth

and two dashes of bitters

Into a shaker toss a cupful of cracked ice. If you are cursed with an automatic ice box crack the cubes up. To this add one part French Vermouth, two parts gin and two dashes of bitters. Place a green olive in each glass and pour. *With this serve:*

SWEDISH CANAPÉS

Mash one cream cheese with a silver fork. To this add one tablespoon of prepared horseradish, six slices of almost burnt bacon, minced, and a pinch of salt. Mix thoroughly and spread on saltines. Dash a little paprika on each for color and serve.

CAVIAR CANAPÉS

Rub a bowl with garlic, cream a little butter in the bowl. Spread thin rounds of white toast with the butter, cover with a layer of black caviar, squeeze a little lemon on each and serve.

"A Pony of Olive Oil is reputed to coat the stomach lining and ameliorate the wear and tear of subsequent beverages . . . A quantity of Moderately Broiled Bacon achieves the same effect."

———⟊⟊⟊———

—◦◦◦—

A Big Evening

If dinner is to be succeeded by bridge, or the theatre, or important amours—in short, if you have any reason to wish to keep yourself or your guest awake, the following combinations are advisable. We are not prepared to give the physiological reasons. Years of experiment, however, have demonstrated that these formulae banish sleep—at least, they do not invite it.

....

DIXON COCKTAIL

Two parts gin

One tablespoon of Scotch

One tablespoon of rye

One part orange juice

and one part pineapple juice (canned)

Shake until very cold and pour into chilled glasses.
With this serve:

....

CHEESE AND CHUTNEY CANAPÉS
Spread rounds of white toast with very finely
chopped chutney, add a layer of Camembert cheese,
and garnish with a thin slice of fresh tomato.

CHEESE AND GHERKIN CANAPÉS

Spread thin strips of fresh bread with cream cheese, to which has been added one-half cup finely chopped salted peanuts and six chopped sweet gherkins.

WATERCRESS SANDWICHES

Cut white bread very thin. Spread plentifully with butter, cover one slice with very crisp leaves of watercress, press firmly together, cut into triangles and serve.

....

PINK LADY COCKTAIL

Two parts gin

One part Grenadine

The juice of one-half lime

and a dash of bitters

Shake vigorously and serve. *With this serve:*

....

MOCK PÂTÉ CANAPÉS

Remove the skin from one-half pound of liver-wurst. Mash it with a fork and add one tablespoon mayonnaise, the juice of half a lemon, half a teaspoon of salt, and a dash of white pepper. Spread generously on wafers or rings of white bread.

ANCHOVY AND CHUTNEY CANAPÉS

Spread rounds of white toast with anchovy butter. Over this spread a layer of finely chopped chutney. Garnish with a bit of pimiento.

SHRIMP AND LIVER SANDWICHES

Chop together one-half cup each of shrimp and cooked chicken livers, one-half Bermuda onion and one-half green pepper. Season with salt and pepper, moisten with mayonnaise. Spread between buttered slices of thin white bread, cut in shapes and serve.

—∽∾∿—

For Virgins

Tender young things, who have just been taken off stick candy, prefer complicated pink and creamy drinks which satisfy their beastly appetite for sweets and at the same time offer an agreeable sense of sinfulness. If you have any crème de menthe or crème de cocoa about the house, make them up some kind of a mess of it and push them under the piano to suck on it. If you don't have these liqueurs, make them up one of the following awful things.

Two canapés are suggested with the Clover Club cocktail, because it is not really bad and can be used for human beings. With the Alexander and Ritz, however, nothing is offered because anyone who would drink them will only sit around and grin, anyway.

....

ALEXANDER COCKTAIL

Into the shaker go

Two parts gin

One part crème de cocoa

One part lime juice

and a pony of thick sweet cream

Add lots of ice and shake violently.

....

....

RITZ COCKTAIL

Two parts gin

One part orange juice

One part pineapple juice

and the beaten white of one egg

This must be shaken until very cold and frothy.

....

....

CLOVER CLUB COCKTAIL

Two parts gin

One part lemon juice

One part orange juice

and the stiffly beaten white of one egg

Shake this until it is very cold. Some demented people add a tablespoon of strained honey, and swear that it is good! *With this serve:*

....

BRIE CANAPÉS

Mix together equal parts of Brie cheese and butter. Spread on a saltine and garnish with one thin slice of stuffed olive.

CAVIARETTES

Filled with caviar (black or pink), seasoned with lemon juice and garnished with the grated white of hard boiled egg, and a dash of paprika.

"Coasters are a snare and a delusion. Besides annoying your guests, they are seldom needed and they complicate life unreasonably."

———∞∞———

—◌◌◌—

Tea Party

Good hostesses will remember the trouble Tea caused in Boston, one of the staidest towns in the world; they will also remember that Tea contains tannin, which is said to be unhygienic, and that the so-called beverage is also reputed to be hard on the teeth.

If, in the face of these considerations, hostesses still insist on endangering the health and well-being of their guests, Heaven at least be with them—the guests will not!

On the whole, it would be better to brew your tea according to some of the splendidly tonic formulae suggested shortly hereafter.

If you are going to have punch for tea, put a large lump of ice in the bowl half an hour before the guests arrive, so that it will be thoroughly chilled. Mix the punch and chill it in the ice-box.

Always place both the punch and the canapés on small, low tables. Otherwise the hungrier guests will crowd around the table, three deep, and the more self-conscious ones will be left to wither and fade in corners.

Never produce too much punch at one time. By the time the guests get down to the bottom the ice will have melted and the liquid will resemble slightly sweetened ice water.

If the punch disappears too rapidly for the ultimate welfare of your party, or for the physical welfare of your guests, serve it yourself and start doing it while those present still have a sense of shame.

If the tea is cocktails serve salt biscuits, dill pickles, potato chips, salted almonds or other standard *hors d'oeuvres*.

SOUTHERN COCKTAIL

Place a Maraschino cherry in a stem goblet. Over this pour one large pony of Bourbon or rye whiskey. Add a dash of Grenadine, one of Benedictine and one of lemon juice.

TENNESSEE COCKTAIL

Two parts of whiskey, one part of Italian Vermouth and a dash of bitters poured over ice and stirred vigorously.

SAZERAC COCKTAIL

Rye whiskey with three dashes each of Anisette, Absinthe and bitters.

PALL MALL COCKTAIL

Rye whiskey with two dashes of Applejack, four dashes of orange juice, two dashes of lemon juice, and two dashes of Grenadine.

EAST INDIAN COCKTAIL

Fill a tall glass with shaved ice. Pour over the ice one teaspoon of raspberry syrup, one teaspoon of Curacao syrup, two dashes of bitters, two dashes of Maraschino and one wine glass of brandy, rye or corn whiskey. Stir well with a spoon and pour into cocktail glasses.

....

JERSEY COCKTAIL

Place three or four cubes of ice in a large glass, add one-half tablespoon of sugar, three dashes of bitters and one wine glass of Applejack. Strain over a twist of lemon peel in each glass.

....

OLD-FASHIONED BACARDI COCKTAIL

Season one glass of Bacardi rum with the juice of one lime and a teaspoon of sugar.

....

OLD-FASHIONED COCKTAIL

These should be made in heavy-bottomed glasses manufactured for the purpose. Into each glass put one lump of sugar, dash a little Angostura Bitters onto the sugar, then crush. Drop one cube of ice into the glass, fill with whiskey (rye or Scotch). Garnish with half a ring of orange, or a twist of lemon peel. Do not stir, but serve with a cocktail or coffee spoon.

RYE AND GRAPEFRUIT JUICE

One part grapefruit juice, two parts rye whiskey, one lump of ice. Stir very gently and drink before it is too cold. One of these taken before breakfast assures one a perfect day.

....

BRANDY COCKTAIL

Into a glass half filled with fine ice pour a wine glass of brandy or corn whiskey, two dashes of Curacao syrup and two dashes of Angostura Bitters. Stir with a spoon and pour into cocktail glasses.

....

———≈∂∂∂≈———

The Big Party

When you owe thousands and thousands of people entertainment, and life's fair prospects have dimmed out in the ungrateful certainty that you are going to have to cook company dinners for years and years, the easy thing is to give a Big Party—in the late afternoon. This method of settling social obligations with one big check need not be completely intolerable. The alternative is to get everyone fairly pie-eyed.

Anyone who gives a Big Party for any other reason than social stress should go back to the land from which he came. Eight people are enough for a Brawl, six for a Riot, and four for Fun. With two guests you can get your bridge played.

If you are entertaining ten or more guests you had better have punch. With enough assistance you can serve cocktails to far more people than this, of course, but your whole evening will be spoiled.

It isn't always necessary to serve sandwiches and canapés at either a Big Party or a Cocktail party. On a table—preferably across the room from the punch bowl, because this keeps the guests in motion and tends toward an Animated Scene—you may arrange several platters of simple comestibles. On one large platter, place a bowl of home-made mayonnaise, banked up to the edge of the platter with shaved ice. On the ice place scores of boiled shrimps—fresh or dry-tinned—from which the spines (they are really their tummies) have been carefully removed.

On another platter of ice have celery stuffed with cream cheese, or Roquefort, or anchovy paste,

72

or caviar, if you happen to be a capitalist. Another platter may hold thin watercress sandwiches, and still another cucumbers which have been cut into eighths, lengthwise, and chilled until they are crisp.

These things are only slightly nourishing and will not interfere with any plans you may have for eating later.

....

FISH HOUSE PUNCH

1 ½ pints of rum (Jamaica preferred)

1 pint of brandy

1 pound of sugar

Juice of 12 lemons

Juice of 6 oranges

and 1 pint of cold tea

Mix these together until the sugar is dissolved. Add one pint of ginger ale, one pint of White Rock and one cup of chopped fresh fruit. Stir thoroughly. Place one large lump of ice in the bowl, and over it pour the punch, very slowly.

....

....

CLARET PUNCH

This punch should be prepared and allowed to stand for half an hour before pouring over the ice and serving.

> 2 quarts of claret, or the local equivalent
>
> 2 pony glasses each of brandy or Applejack, and Benedictine syrup
>
> 3 slices of orange
>
> 3 slices of pineapple
>
> 1 small bottle of Maraschino cherries
>
> 3 long slices of fresh cucumber rind

Put one large piece of ice in the bowl, allowing just enough room at the sides for dipping with the ladle. Strain the punch over the ice, and allow it to stand ten minutes before dipping it into the punch cups.

....

....

GIN PUNCH NUMBER ONE

2 quarts of gin

2 quarts of grapefruit juice

and one-quarter cup of Five Fruits
or Grenadine

Keep the punch in the ice box for two hours before serving time, so that it will be thoroughly chilled. Pour over chopped ice in the bowl and serve at once.

....

....

GIN PUNCH NUMBER TWO

26 cocktail glasses of gin

55 glasses of Orgeat syrup
(buy at any chemist's shop)

5 glasses lemon juice

and 5 glasses of orange juice

Chill for two hours before serving. Pour over chopped ice in the punch bowl.

....

....

MILK PUNCH

This should be made in a cocktail shaker. One-half glass of fine ice, one wine glass of brandy, one wine glass of rum, and half a glass of rich milk. Shake thoroughly, strain into a tall glass, dust with grated nutmeg and serve.

....

BRANDY PUNCH

In a large bar glass stir one-half tablespoon of sugar, a few drops of raspberry syrup, half a tea-spoon of lemon juice and one-half glass of water. Fill the glass with shaved ice, pour over it one and a half wine glasses of brandy. Strain well and strain into another cold glass.

....

....

PORT WINE PUNCH

Stir well together, one-half tablespoon of sugar, one-half tablespoon of orange juice, half a teaspoon of lemon juice, and one-half wine glass of water. Fill a glass with shaved ice, and pour over it one and one-half wine glasses of port wine or the best available substitute. Garnish with fresh fruit and serve with a straw.

....

....

ROMAN PUNCH

In a large glass dissolve one-half pony glass of raspberry syrup and three dashes of lemon juice in half a wine glass of water. Fill the glass with shaved ice, and over it pour one wine glass of brandy, one-half pony of rum, and one-half pony of Curacao. Stir well, garnish with fresh fruit and serve with a straw.

....

EGG MILK PUNCH

Shake together until the mixture is creamy, one slightly beaten egg, one-half tablespoon of sugar, one cup of shaved ice, one wine glass of brandy, one pony of rum and half a table glass of good rich milk. Strain into glasses and dust with grated nutmeg.

....

....

WHISKEY PUNCH

Fill a tall glass one-third full of very finely crushed ice, add two teaspoons of sugar and stir well. Add the juice of one-half lemon, then a little more ice. Over this pour one wine glass of whiskey. Stir constantly, while adding a tablespoon of ice at a time, until the glass is full. The glasses will be frosted on the outside. Dust lightly with powdered sugar and drink. This is a famous old Southern drink.

....

"If one or more of your guests arrives after the others are already playing London Bridge or Patty-cake, snake them to the kitchen and get them off to a good start."

———ᔕᔕᔕ———

—◦◦◦—

Catching Up

If one or more of your guests arrives after the others are already playing London Bridge or Patty-cake, snake them to the kitchen and get them off to a good start.

If you attempt to do this by mere volume, the effects will be lamentable. The mechanisms which are supposed to transport the refined alcohol to the brain will at first merely curl up with low moans. Later, bucked up by the surrounding stimulant, they will awaken and begin functioning in a big way. At about the time you bring on the roast, the belated guest will begin jumping up and down on the ceiling in a playful manner.

The thing to do is to give the late-comer a moderate dose but in heated form. Heat acts on the villi and such things like an air-mail stamp. Hence the following:

CATCHING UP

....

I

A stiff hooker of gin with the juice of half a lemon and a little hot water. (Too much hot water induces a healthy perspiration and nullifies the effect.)

II

Half and half, hot water and rye or Scotch. This takes full effect in ten minutes. Serve in a tea-cup, about three-quarters full for an average customer.

III

In hot weather, a tumbler of equal parts grape-fruit juice and gin—just enough ice to make the combination palatable.

Bottle for a Certain Purpose

For the boy who, after one drink, wants to drink all the liquor he can hold and then pour any possible surplus in his hair, the wise host will construct and place in a conspicuous part of the kitchen, The Bottle For a Certain Purpose. This consists of 10 per cent non-alcoholic alcohol, two drops gin extract, aqua pura to fill. Mix in the most obvious gin bottle available.

By the time your guest is avid enough to invade the kitchen he won't know the difference. A shot or two of Tabasco will make this even more deceptive, but leave the bottle uncorked until the peppery smell departs.

"Try to impress upon your subconscious that you must not go to sleep or bed while your head is whirling. The penalty is a marvelous hangover."

Emergency

If one of your guests, rather the better for drink, should be called upon suddenly to preach a sermon in the Cathedral of St. John the Divine, or attend a meeting of Congress, or speak before the W. C. T. U., try black coffee on him first of all, adding, if he seems flushed, a teaspoon of aromatic spirits of ammonia.

If this is ineffectual, give further a dose of—

One rounded teaspoon of bicarbonate of soda, one teaspoon of aromatic spirits of ammonia, in a tumbler of carbonated water. Stir well.

A well-tried theatre remedy is one tablespoon of Worcestershire Sauce in a wine glass of water. If the patient is an ingenue of delicate constitution, four strong men will be able to hold her while the dose is being administered.

The one disadvantage of this remedy is that, though the subject will be able to get through her lines for about an hour, at the end of that time she will discover definite symptoms of *mal de mer*. However, she will be out of your house by that time.

---◦◦◦---

Plumbing Fixtures

The weariest thing in the world is to make the long trek between the bed of pain and the bathroom only to find that the green depths of the Acid Acetylsalicylic bottle are as empty as Life's fair promises of the previous evening.

If you are a Guest, take a potion from any of the small bottles marked with a skull and crossbones. This will occasion your hosts enough embarrassment to ensure their reform. They may even be hanged, if you arrange things cleverly, which is the Ideal, of course.

If it is your own home, check your bathroom commissary by the following list, at the first presages of a party:

Bathroom Commissary List

1 bottle 100 aspirin tablets.

1 pint or more lime water.

1 large bottle Fruit Salts.

1 flacon ammoniac smelling salts.

1 large bottle aromatic spirits of ammonia.

1 tin bicarbonate of soda.

1 bottle milk of magnesia.

1 bottle mercurochrome (for wounds).

1 bottle rubbing alcohol (for sprains or severe contusions).

The lime water, if gargled after the teeth are brushed,
will make the interior of the mouth quite inhabitable.

—◈◈◈—

Hot Weather Drinks

There is no known way of avoiding summer. Even at the North Pole it gets above freezing in the month of August—or perhaps it was January, the Poles are so contrary—and so the best thing to do is to drink beverages which will encourage metabolism and furnish an illusion, at least momentary, of autumnal comfort.

The drinks consist of Juleps, Highballs and Rickeys, and also the magnificent John Collins, whoever he was.

JOHN COLLINS

In the bottom of a tall glass put one teaspoon of sugar and a few dashes of fresh lemon juice. Add three or four pieces of ice and one wine glass of gin. Fill the glass with soda water, stir very gently, so that the soda does not foam up in the glass, remove the ice and drink.

GIN FIZZ

Into a highball glass put one-half tablespoon of powdered sugar and four or five dashes of fresh lemon juice. Fill the glass with finely shaved ice and pour over it one wine glass of gin. Stir thoroughly and drain the liquid off into another tall glass. Fill up with seltzer or Vichy.

....

SILVER FIZZ

Put the beaten white of one egg, half a tablespoon of powdered sugar and four dashes of lemon juice into a tall glass. Fill the glass with shaved ice, over which pour one wine glass of gin. Stir thoroughly and drain the liquid into another highball glass. Fill up with seltzer or Vichy.

....

GOLDEN FIZZ

Mix the yolk of one egg, well beaten, with one wine glass of gin or whiskey, add one teaspoon of powdered sugar and four dashes of lemon. Fill the glass with seltzer or Vichy.

....

GIN FIX

One-half tablespoon of powdered sugar, four dashes of lemon or lime juice and one-half pony of pineapple juice in a tall glass. Half fill the glass with shaved ice. Add a wine glass of gin, stir well, garnish with fresh fruit and serve with a straw.

JOE RICKEY

Squeeze one-half lime into a tall glass and drop in the rind. Add two wine glasses of Bourbon or rye whiskey, stir thoroughly, fill up with seltzer or plain water and drop in one small lump of ice.

....

GIN RICKEY

Squeeze one-half lime into a tall glass and drop in the rind. Add one wine glass of gin, stir thoroughly, fill the glass with seltzer water and drop in one lump of ice.

....

MINT JULEP

Dissolve one teaspoon of sugar in a little water in the bottom of a tall glass. Add a few sprigs of fresh mint and stir so as to crush the leaves slightly. Remove the mint. Add one and a half ponies of brandy, or whiskey, and fill the glass with shaved ice. Stir until cold and put a sprig of mint on top. You may drink this through a straw or bury your nose in the foliage.

....

GIN AND GINGER ALE

Put some cracked ice in a tall glass. Over this
pour one—or two or three—ponies of gin. Fill the
glass with ginger ale and add a dash of lemon or bitters. Stir thoroughly.

GIN AND WHITE ROCK

Dissolve one teaspoon of sugar in a little water
in the bottom of a tall glass. Add two dashes of lemon. Fill the glass half full of chopped ice, and add
the White Rock. And, oh yes, some gin.

WHISKEY AND SODA

Pour a shot of Scotch whiskey into a glass, and

fill the glass up with soda water, being careful to syphon it slowly. Do not use ice in this drink.

....

COBBLERS

This drink may be made of anything from Italian Red Ink to champagne from the same general formula.

....

SHERRY COBBLER

In a large glass dissolve one-half tablespoon of sugar with one-half wine glass of water. Fill the glass with very fine shaved ice. Over this pour enough Sherry to reach the top. Garnish with fresh fruits and serve with a straw.

....

"Always take cheer from the thought that if you are healthy enough to suffer acutely, you will probably live."

Cold Weather Drinks

Toddies and other drinks listed hereafter are not for evenings of what is now called Serious Drinking. But they will do excellently to start such an evening of endeavor, after a day of hunting, fishing, skating, skiing, tobogganing, or shopping in the rain.

As you drink one of the following delectable combinations, consider the poor victims of the wintry Alps, who have to get along with straight Benedictine, transported by large and hairy dogs.

WHISKEY TODDY

In a whiskey glass dissolve one-half teaspoon of sugar in a little water, add one piece of ice and a wine glass of whiskey. Stir.

BRANDY TODDY

Dissolve one-half teaspoon of sugar in half a whiskey glass of water. Add one lump of ice, and a wine glass of brandy (any kind), and stir. Remove the ice before serving.

WHISKEY SOUR

Dissolve one-half tablespoon of sugar in a little soda water. Add the juice of one-quarter lemon. Fill the glass with crushed ice and pour over it one wine glass of whiskey. Stir well with a spoon and garnish with any fruit. If it is used for a pick-me-up dispense with the fruit.

....

HOT SCOTCH SLING

In a heavy whiskey glass dissolve one lump of sugar in a little hot water. To this add a wine glass of Scotch whiskey and a little lemon peel. Fill the glass with hot water, dust a little nutmeg on top and serve.

....

HOT GIN SLING

Dissolve one-half loaf of sugar in a little hot water, add two dashes of lemon juice, pour in one wine glass of gin and fill the glass with very hot water.

....

....

HOT SPICED RUM

Dissolve one lump of sugar and one-half tea-spoon of mixed allspice in a little hot water in the bottom of an old-fashioned whiskey glass. Add one wine glass of rum and fill the glass with hot water. Stir and dust a little grated nutmeg on top. A lump of butter added to this drink is excellent for sore throats and colds.

....

HOT LEMONADE

In a tall thick glass stir one tablespoon of sugar and the juice of half a lemon. To this add a pony of whiskey, rum or gin, fill the glass with boiling water and stir.

....

....

HOT RUM

Dissolve one loaf of sugar in a little hot water, in a thick table glass. Add one wine glass of rum (any kind) and fill the glass with boiling water.

....

CAFÉ ROYALE

Equal parts of strong hot coffee and whiskey or rum.

....

---❦---

The Yuletide Bowl

For the Christmas or New Year at Home, egg-nog has long been the accepted beverage. It is a nuisance to make and has to be very carefully prepared, but perhaps it is worth it. The following formula is for two gallons of egg-nog.

Separate the yolks from the whites of twenty very fresh eggs. Beat the yolks until they are as thin as water. Add two pounds of pulverized sugar and stir thoroughly. Put the mixture in the punch bowl and add two quarts of brandy, and one and one-half pints of rum (St. Croix is the old accepted rum). To this, stirring constantly and pouring very slowly to prevent curdling, add one and one-half gallons of rich milk.

Beat the whites of the eggs until very stiff and place in little islands on top of the punch. Dust generously with grated nutmeg. When serving, ladle out two-thirds of a punch cup of the yellow punch and place a little of the white on top of each cup.

Serve only sweet biscuits or very thin sand cookies with egg-nog.

This Page Removed at the request of the United States Attorney for the Southern District of New York.

*The following section contains the restored page from the original 1930 edition.

Household Hints

For making non-alcoholic gin, the following formula, which your druggist will fill for you, supplies the best flavoring:

Juniper, 24 drops; angelica, 2 drops; anise, 1 drop; tincture of sweet orange, 2 drops. Have these ingredients mixed in a two-ounce bottle, and fill the bottle with non-alcoholic (you ass) alcohol, before measuring the drops for the following process.

Use one part non-alcoholic alcohol to two parts water. Thus—for a quart of non-alcoholic gin, take 1 1/3 cups non-alcoholic alcohol, 6 drops of flavoring mixture described above, and 1½ teaspoons glycerine, and shake together. Then add 2 2/3 cups distilled water.

The longer these elements are allowed to stand in a loosely corked bottle, the more intimate and amiable they will become.

Before retiring in a Bad Way, always take a large dose of Fruit Salts or other effervescent laxative. If there is any tendency toward nausea it should be assiduously cultivated at this time; it will be more painful in the morning.

Experiences differ on aspirin taken before retiring. That is something everyone must learn for himself.

Try to impress upon your subconscious that you must not go to sleep or bed while your head is whirling. The penalty is a marvelous hangover. Drink quantities of water and hot coffee and keep moving; take violent exercise if you can. An extremely hot bath is also recommended, though it induces drowsiness.

Another successful antidote for imprudent absorption is a series of long and very deep breaths. Fill your lungs completely, but rather slowly. The amount of alcohol one can work off in this way is amazing.

For hiccups: First, of course, a drink of water. Then, if necessary, the traditional ten slow sips. Finally, the Aesculapian remedy of holding the breath as long as is conveniently possible. This device is assisted if, while holding your breath, you think profoundly of someone you hate violently.

**"Total Unconsciousness
is not the goal of Perfect
Drinking."**

Comes the Dawn

That drink is deceptive was noted many, many evenings ago, so that it is not necessary to do more here than call your attention to the fact that even the soberest of men will sometimes wake up and wonder what hit them after the second highball. If, after a long sleep, he judges that it was the Himalaya Mountains, he had better take two aspirin tablets with a tablespoon of hot water, chewing the tablets before swallowing. (I know it's nasty, Mama's Precious, but so is bad old headache.)

After a lapse of fifteen or twenty minutes, he should take, slowly, the following breakfast:

1. A Little of the Hair of the Dog that Bit Him.

2. One pint of milk.

3. A half-pint of sauerkraut or tomato juice.

4. A cup of black coffee to which has been added one teaspoon of spirits of ammonia.

If the case is not so serious, consisting merely of a slightly dazed feeling and a suggestion of a headache, after some Fruit Salts, or other mild and prompt cathartic, a hot and cold shower, and a toothbrush, take the following:

MORNING GLORY FIZZ

Mix together in a highball glass, half a teaspoon of sugar, three dashes of lemon juice, three dashes of lime juice, three dashes of Absinthe, if obtainable, otherwise Angostura Bitters, the beaten white of one egg, a wine glass of Scotch, a lump or two of ice. Fill the tumbler with Vichy or other effervescent water, stir until cold and drink quickly.

This settles the nerves and creates an appetite. A hearty breakfast of hot cereal and bacon, or three-minute (no more) eggs and bacon, or toast and marmalade, all with hot black coffee, completes the treatment.

If the case is more serious, however, a Prairie Oyster is a good kill or cure remedy. This consists of a raw egg drowned in Worcestershire Sauce. More conservative treatment for a sour stomach, heartburn, or other unfavorable manifestations of an alimentary nature are the following:

For heartburn, one-half tablespoon of soda in a short tumbler of soda water.

For an exceedingly hot spot at the back of the stomach, apparently involving the spine, milk of magnesia.

For a sore stomach, caused by eating too soon after or too shortly before drinking, a good strong cathartic, of an immediate nature.

For legitimate nausea, milk and lime water. (And see what happens.)

For fruitless nausea, almost any strongly effervescent drink, such as sal hepatica, Fruit Salts, baking soda in a glass of water strongly tinctured with lime or lemon juice—these to be sipped while smelling a bottle of ammoniac smelling salts, or spirits of ammonia.

Ammonia is prescribed in all cases of throbbing headache. It steadies the heart. It is excellent for that form of katzenjammer in which the head seems to have been stuffed full of warm mud, also. In fact, ammonia, inhaled and imbibed, is a good bet for everything. The doses are so minute that there is virtually no chance that it will harm the patient.

The citrates and other *ites* and *ates* which are commonly recommended are fine things to let alone, unless you or your physician knows what you are doing.

Always take cheer from the thought that if you are healthy enough to suffer acutely, you will probably live.

Lots of rot is talked about remedies. If some of these don't cure you, there is nothing left except Blowing the Brain Out or *De Consolatione Philosophiae*.

———

Other Recipes

....

....

....

....

....

....

....

....

....

....

Idiosyncrasies of
Your Friends

....

....

....

....

....

....

....

....

....

....

The work of illustrator **HERB ROTH** (1887–1953) graced newspapers and magazines in the first half of the twentieth century, as well as books by Robert Benchley, David Ogden Stewart, and others. He lived in New York City and Del Ray Beach, Florida.